Networking
... a guide

Networking
... a guide

Copyright Charlie Kenny 2015

All rights reserved

Photography courtesy Gibson-Phillips
www.gisphotographic.co.uk

Layout and Design by Nudge Creative Design LLP
NudgeCreativeDesign.com

Produced and published by

GO! Publicity.me (UK)
Hertfordshire and Northumberland
Telephone. 01665 577084
charliekenny.wordpress.com

Dedicated to an old friend.

Contents

About the author 7

Introduction to the booklet 9

Why networking 13

Where do I start 19

Getting to know you 25

Help your network 29

The opportunity 33

Your presentation 37

The referral 39

The Weekly Business agenda/about 42

Guidelines 45

The one to one 48

When the Baker met the Lawyer 51

About the author

Charlie Kenny is founder and regular host to The Weekly Business network forum, established January 2010.

Charlie was born in Lincolnshire and emigrated to Australia at an early age. He was raised in Perth, Western Australia before moving with family to Sydney where he finished High School. He began training for a diploma in Media & Design with Sungravure, a Fairfax Group News subsidiary, qualifying after four years. A short spell working at the Sydney Morning Herald followed before embarking on a period of extensive travel.

In 1985 Charlie returned to the UK and soon established his own print and design company providing broad-based services to a variety of organisations located throughout the South-East of England. In 1999 he transformed the business, providing a bespoke publishing and publicity service.

Over the years Charlie has gained much experience by participating in the many different styles of 'Networking' (the good and the not so good,) with personal referrals being something that have greatly contributed to the development of his own business.

Charlie Kenny lives with family at Howick, Nr Alnwick, Northumberland.

> *"You can have everything in life you want, if you just help enough other people get what they want."*
>
> ~ Zig Ziglar

Introduction

This handbook is not about something I feel you have to do nor is it something I feel you need to be doing or even about what you should be doing in pursuit of better business. That would simply not work would it?

The information found within the pages of this booklet is meant to offer guidance and support. Much of the material has been gleaned during my own networking, some of it is original, some is borrowed, most of it is simply common sense.

The Weekly Business is about belonging. Once you better understand where you feel like you belong, where you fit, you know that you can serve people better. People either get you or they don't. They know what you're into or they don't.

There's less friction when you belong. There's less grey. There is less "fuss."

We're all different, although very similar.

The aim of this booklet is firstly to introduce our Business Forum and secondly to give you an idea of how you can make a difference if you really wish to pursue the psychology of buying into people.

"If I can help enough others get what they want ..." yes, I know, you've heard it all before although I really do believe that prosperity comes our way if while pursuing our passion we help one another along the way.

OK, so bear with me, "back in the day" I was spending

a lot of my time travelling, I was forever on the road visiting customers and potential clients. Fifty percent of my time was sitting in maddening amounts of traffic, no mobile communication available either 'back then,' this was well before digital and the ubiquitous 'mobile' became the must-have sales accessory!

It is my opinion that the value of the noble art of relationship building is today generally overlooked or in some instances it's value has become a hollow representation of what it once was.

These days every man and his dog is an expert in just about everything in a world seemingly obsessed with further (and further!) education, certification and qualification to define each as the go-to 'expert in their field.' It appears that nowadays, experience amounts for very little and that most valuable education ('schooling of life') seems to have been sadly overlooked.

Or has it?

Even without the luxury of digital communications I was lucky enough to spend the other half of my former working life in front of customers who were looking forward to my regular visits, who wished to hear about my products and services and preferred me being around in person to offer advice in support of their business, at the best possible prices. My opinion mattered, my experience was of value, In the eyes of my prospect, I had integrity.

'Doing business' meant more than convenience, a purchase order or a necessary selection from the forthcoming new product list. Many of the aforementioned customers also became my friends and some remain to this day.

Over time I soon came to understand that people do indeed buy from people and I truly believe that personal engagement is an extremely valuable part of business.

With the advent of new technology and by learning to 'work smart' the time I now spend sitting in traffic is minimal and I'm more likely to be found networking or at home with family – or even sat in front of a keyboard!

I trust that you find this handbook useful.

"Networking is about marketing, marketing yourself and what you stand for."

~ The Weekly Business

Why networking?

You know how it is. Many of us hurry through life going from one place to the next, focused on conquering the next mountain, making the next deal or chasing the day-to-day stuff and believing that we will never have enough time to do all the things we need to get done. Yet, there is all the time in the world if we just take a minute to realise that we are the creators of this life, the life we choose to live.

Life is a series of choices and being free from any stress is one of those choices we can make.

Whether your business life is overly complicated or your personal life a mess (or both), you have chosen this current system of chaos. The world can be totally hurly-burly with a never ending offer of the next 'fix' for this or the solution for that. More and more 'stuff' with more people and processes with their own demands arrive into our lives both professionally and personally. We are so busy being busy, it's easy to be lured into the routine, creating those lengthy to-do lists, which can be daunting in themselves, not to mention extremely stressful.

It can be tough being you. Especially when we are working for ourselves, or in charge of our own journey whilst working from a remote work-place destination.

The greatest achievements have often come from the simplest of ideas and in the simplest of forms. To experience a more simplified life, we must first learn to slow down long enough to enable us to see through the clutter.

Think clarity

Networking, given the 'right for you' structured environment, at a venue that is comfortable for you and your business can help you with clarity. Once you have found you are at ease in your network and your environment you must learn to demonstrate that you are likewise comfortable in the shoes you wear.

People like to do business with people who are calming, in control and who offer stability in a supportive environment. We like to do business with those we know and with those we trust, business is much better with friends isn't it?

Once you have spent some time with like-minded people in an environment that is removed from the office and/or the day-to-day routine you soon begin to understand that 'stress' is able to be put aside, put down for a bit and in some instances not picked up again at all. The magic is that the support network that is your network of trusted colleagues offers not only **clarity of thought** but insights into what were once (in your mind at least) certain dark clouds on the horizon, now dispelled through networking, by engagement.

Think Referral

Of course it is not only the support network that some are looking for through networking, there are other benefits as well, namely referral. The referred lead is typically a much better quality prospect than someone you've never met or spoken with in the past, someone with who you have nothing in common.

The **referred business prospect**, therefore someone who has been recommended, been given your details and who is awaiting your call, also comes with the following benefits:
* The referred prospect is generally easier to close (less stress!)
* She/he has less gripes or complaints
* Almost always returns for more business
* Is more trusting and most importantly ...
* Is more likely to refer you on to his/her contacts

Generally speaking, when participating and building relationships through regular networking, with the clarity and insights we quickly gather, business can be a more pleasant experience, more profitable and less stressful.

Referrals are certainly a great **by-product** of networking, of association, with new business a distinct possibility at little or no cost. By comparison, cold calling, which almost all of us dislike, can waste an enormous amount of time for little reward. Advertising, even when strategically focused is in relative terms inefficient when compared to a single referral which can bring in a whole host of future business as the original satisfied customer endorses you to his closest allies who in turn inform their own contacts.

> The great bonus of referrals? It is of course, 'positive' business. It's new opportunity with ATTITUDE, it's about new prospects who have heard good things about you and who trust you through association. PLUS, through their own choice, the prospect is already warm to your business.

Cultivation is the key

Networking is not for everyone; of course we know that's true. We all have our set routines, our comfort zones and for many, to implement change in our already full and busy lives is to create havoc. But, and this is a really powerful 'but,' if you wish to engage others, see the value in knowledge transfer, in developing partnerships with like minded individuals who represent a diversity that you do not have already in your world, you should not dismiss what, over time the structured network offers you.

The key to successful referral marketing is the relationship. Cultivating the engagement with others, your visibility, your ability to offer information and support, presenting your 'offer' amongst peers and not forgetting those referrals you generate for others in business as well as for yourself, all of these elements have everything to do with relationships.

Partnerships remember, are a two way street and referral marketing is no different. We need to work smart for all parties concerned to benefit and to become successful.

Not forgetting - we remember those who help us don't we? We enjoy talking them up, it makes us feel good.

Let's take a minute and remind ourselves whom it is we have always turned to for help. Perhaps when we've found ourselves out of a job, short of cash or struggling with advice - who do we call for advice, direction or to get to the job done? Those close friends from our trusted contacts list, right?

Networking is not the 'quick fix'

The structured referral network is not so good for those looking for a quick fix to a fundamental business problem. If your business is in dire straits, or the liquidators are at your door I would suggest that you seek specialist support.

Networking is not so good for 'The Hunter' either, those of us in business wishing to pick up a an order here and there or simply looking to leave the cards in the hope of a 'chance.' Structured referral networking is not ideal for this type of business operator and I would suggest an open community network 'mixer' or seasonal trade show might better suit the hunter mentality.

> *"Joint undertakings stand a better chance when they benefit both sides."*
>
> ~ Euripides

I'm in, so where do I start?

We have many opportunities to help ourselves and colleagues produce better business.

The referral isn't always obvious and it depends entirely on which trade or service each of us provide, although for quality referrals, like most things of value we need to commit time to nurture trust or the business opportunity to take place.

We need to be there or if you cannot 'be there' in person, why ask someone from outside your Forum to represent you? Networking for referral is not a long distance business affair; we're not cold calling. Your Business Forum is not a social media platform either we're about people engagement and about learning, building a community.

To realise the opportunity, each of us need to reprise the engagement, educate and repeat on a regular basis. Relationships take time to develop, your business is an entity that changes as we ourselves change and it's important to enlighten our colleagues on what it is we are good at, where we work, what we do and how we do it.

So where to start? Hone the offer, your presentation, your one minute snap-shot, elevator pitch, hip-shot delivery, whatever you like to call it. Be clear, precise and make it notable. Try not to deliver every service or solution that you and the company provide, it will almost certainly spoil the effectiveness of presentation and confuse your listening, your potential sales team. Give your listeners a reason to buy in and sell on your behalf.

Try and be specific, think *"needs for now"* or even ask for a name you'd like to connect with, a location for a business or perhaps a lead into a current trend. We should certainly be sure about what we are asking for so that colleagues see our expertise and are able to introduce us with ease.

Toward the back of this handbook you will find an example of what your short pitch presentation might entail. Remember, you usually only have about 60 seconds (depending on the size of the audience) on any given day and therefore we should keep the delivery salient.

Ok, we've started with the importance of regular appearances, introductions, relationships and familiarity that are the cornerstone of building the trust and the all important referral process.

So, what's next?

Consider introducing a guest

Bringing a guest along to your network Forum is a fantastic way to help everyone in the network. The visitor brings a whole host of new connections list and of course down the line with those new connections, come referral.

Our business Forum thrives on diversity, the supportive attitude and enthusiasm. So any new visitor to our network is welcome – as long as there is a 'complementary fit' amongst the specialists already cultivating business in the room and that we are not duplicating those skills.

The new face, visiting for the first time, full of expectation and bringing an offer of skills until now not evident within the group adds a whole new dimension. It is well documented that each of us know hundreds of personal contacts, perhaps thousands, therefore with a new face in the room, **the potential market** that our specific referral request (or message) reaches is hugely magnified.

Some new attendees doubt they are able to introduce anyone to the Forum. This is only natural, especially when we are coming to grips with a concept, that for many is completely alien. It is sometimes difficult enough to contend with our own change of business dimension. Change is good though.

It will take some time to grow the confidence in what your Forum can offer before you introduce your own contacts, for some the enthusiasm for their Forum is irresistible and through this enthusiasm alone word of mouth referral is at work. We like to offer help, we already know that and it certainly depends on your contact sphere although once you become settled and you learn who is in the room and what their particular needs are, inviting comes a little easier. For some, over time it becomes routine when they see just how much a new face impacts the Forum.

Time to grow - with the 'one to one'

So often overlooked as *'why should I bother, they know me already'* the one to one (121) is a great way to hasten your understanding of what it is your colleagues actually provide. It may be that the short (60 second) presentation is just part of their offer and that they are unable (during the formal part of the meeting) to mention certain skills or services through courtesy and respect of other specialists present in the room.

With the 121 **we dig a little deeper.** Therefore spend time off-site (or on site), with colleagues over a coffee, in the pub or over a meal, whenever time is available. The 121 meetings are a proven way to consolidate the understanding that is so vital in empowering others to offer referrals. All of us should aim to take time and meet our 'sales team' on a regular basis. After all, this is what our colleagues become through cultivation over time, ambassadors for our business.

Even those we don't believe that even in a million years we'd be able to find leads for, let alone referrals can bring us a whole batch of new opportunities if we simply offer to spend time discovering the common ground until now unseen.

Take centre stage with an extended presentation

Every now and then you will find that you are presented with the opportunity to educate with more of an insight to yourself and your business through 'the extended presentation.' This is **a valuable time**, a fantastic complement to your regular **60-second presentation** and should be taken with gusto! Usually consisting of around 10 minutes although it depends on the numbers attending any given meeting.

Take the opportunity with both hands. Be yourself by showing you are human and by ... engaging! Then once you have completed your presentation, be sure to re-book, keep the ball going and ensure the message stays fresh because the more exposure your network offers is great for the ... Bizability!

PLEASE BE AWARE! Technology plays a great part in our lives and many understandably like to offer the extended presentation through power point or slide share. Now we all know how much a picture sells ... a million words right? Maybe so, although if the technology is not up to the job, it can be frustrating for everyone, let alone you the presenter.

It is always wise to enlist back-up in the shape of a 'lovely assistant' working with you, ensuring that you are both in sync with the working presentation so that if things do happen to go awry with technology, a worthy contingency plan is in place or you are able to deliver without the technology if possible.

PRESENTATION TIP ... Some make the mistake of handing out paper at the start of a presentation. Please avoid doing so. This practice will defer the focus of your audience from you to the paperwork with the result being a good proportion of your listeners will not 'hear' your message at all. You only have a short time, make it count, ask for any questions to wait until you've finished and save any detail regarding the 'bigger picture' until the aforementioned 121.

ONE MORE THING ... Your Chairperson is in the room to help you, as indeed your network colleagues are. If you need guidance regard timing, presentation tips, set up or stimulus, please simply ask.

> *"You never know when you're going to get an opportunity."*
>
> ~ Dwight Henry

Getting to know you, really know you

The process of developing and building relations is unique to every pair of individuals and of course every business. It takes time and as the relationship grows there are three definitive phases, certainly during the early days of the networking experience or even when assessing the progress of engagement to date.

Three distinct phases of growth:

1) Visibility

To develop our foundations for success we first need to be seen. In business this may be through advertising or PR efforts or perhaps through a mutual friend who has observed the way you work and the functionality of your business, your service or product. Once you become recognised as a reputable business the relationship starts to flourish with more people becoming interested in your 'offer.'

Our referral partners have great potential to promote our business, spreading the word as they go. Progressing to the second level, one of credibility, the level of visibility must be maintained; we cannot aspire to be successful while standing still.

> *"Be not afraid of growing slowly; be only afraid of standing still."*
> ~ Chinese proverb.

2) Credibility

By continuing to strive for recognition though visibility we soon attain a level of reliable worth and confidence in the marketplace. Our peers gravitate toward us and we each start to form opinions and expectations of one other. Fulfilment takes place with these relationships entering a certain level of understanding and satisfaction, knowing that we are able to continue the process of growth in consolidation of credibility. Demonstrating who we are, doing as we say, delivering on promises and going the extra mile. You will find that others within your circle, those who have not worked with you or your company as yet turn to their own peers seeking confirmation of your ability to deliver.

> *"Trust is built on credibility and credibility comes from acting in others' interests before our own."*
> ~ Stephen Denny

3) Profitability

Any mature relationship, whether business or personal can be defined in terms of its profitability. Is the partnership working? Does the business bear fruit for both parties, are we satisfied, therefore is the relationship mutually beneficial? If it is not, then the relationship will not last. It is not easy to forecast when particular business relationships become profitable, for some it is almost overnight, for others it may take considerably longer, months perhaps, even years. It certainly depends on the quality of contacts and the participants efforts of visibility in gaining credibility.

Depending on who is listening you may find you are suddenly very busy managing expectation while just days beforehand you were consumed simply by being seen. Real profitability is certainly not found in bargain hunting, we need to embrace the cultivators mentality, much like farming, it takes time to build skills and therefore plenty of patience is required.

Concentrating on building the contacts through your network, those who realise you are that credible, go to person worthy of recommendation is the key to becoming profitable. As we work the visibility we are not only sending the message out to our most obvious next best customer but also far further a-field with news reaching many unseen observers who just may be working on our behalf.

> *"Be seen, cultivate the credible to realise the profitable"*
> ~ Anon

> *"One loyal friend is worth ten thousand relatives."*
>
> ~ Euripides

Help your network help you

It's exciting times ahead when you decide to make the concerted effort and spend time developing the referral opportunity. Word of mouth recommendation is hardly a new experience; we've been doing that for a long time now although today, networking amongst trusted colleagues has become an essential part of the marketing mix.

So we find we are committed to spending some time working on growth. How do I get my colleagues to find me business?

First of all you should ask yourself, '*do they know what I want?*' Time spent educating your audience via clear messages of support, offering information and developing the partnerships are key.

Networking works in the same way as you would solve dilemmas for your family, friends, confidantes or anyone else in need of help. We first need to find out how we can help who needs what and then talk 'em up!

How to help each other

There are many ways to empower others. The important thing is to start the process of engagement. Here are some ways to help your colleagues help you:

Get to know your referral partners. The best way to learn who is most likely to help you with referrals is to sit down and spend time listening. Find out more about each other.

Book a one to one meeting, either on the day

of the meeting or off-site to perhaps discuss the circles you move in, professional and personal interests plus of course any common ground. There have been plenty of strategic partnerships started through the effective one to one (121).

Introduce your Forum to a new face at your meeting. They are, after all the life-blood for new business. A fantastic opportunity for everyone it is true and especially good for any colleague who has been hinting at a particular trade or service they would like to meet. This has a great reciprocal effect and does your credibility no harm at all.

Ask your friends to **include your sales material** to their own offer, perhaps include your leaflet inside own brochure? Even better, if they have a shop window, ask them to post your card or leaflet up for passers-by to see.

Is there anyone in your Forum attending **an upcoming event**? Why not ask if you can get a lift and accompany them? Again, it can be a great one to one opportunity.

Are you doing any **community work**? If so, ask your Referral partner to mention this during open networking, this adds gravitas to your offer, people like to hear about community support from one of their own, it's also a great reflection on your local Forum.

Why not produce some alternative cards and include a **'limited time offer?'** Then ask your colleagues to pass the cards to friends and family. It's another great way of identifying those able to work with you developing the referral partnerships. These days short run printing is not expensive, even if printed both sides and why waste the advertising space?

Have a **social media presence**? Ask friends to give your offer a mention on Twitter perhaps, a like on Facebook or share on LinkedIn. More social activity is a great way to bolster the visibility. Work together to help each other.

Leads are good. It's always great when you've spent days, weeks, sometimes months educating and presenting to your colleagues and along comes an offer to *'someone I know who may be interested.'* It confirms that you are making headway and that the message is working.

Referrals are better. Lets assume the same 'offer' comes along although worded something like this *'someone I know may be interested in your offer, I've passed them your card and they are waiting to hear from you. Do you think you could give them a call please?'*

The Raving Fan

Here's more. Ask the person who offered you the above lead to **qualify the need and produce a referral**. Instead of accepting a lead, ask your partner to pass further information on to the interested party, perhaps your offer of a no obligation meeting or news of who you are working with just now. Ask your referral partner to sell for you – after all, they know the prospect better than you and it's a great lesson for anyone when building the network – a lead is a start, but a referral, business that is waiting for you after an introduction from a 'raving fan,' is much better.

> *"Networking is an opportunity, nothing more."*
>
> ~ Anon

Networking is an opportunity

The Weekly Business offer regular meetings of like-minded people in an environment that encourages a level field of individual participation in pursuit of alliance and the enhanced business opportunity or referral.

> *"An introduction to someone who is in the market for your product or services, who has been given your details and is expecting your call."*

We've covered the basic practices in previous pages although it is worth noting that turning up is just the start. Here is my top six for your personal check list:

Top 6 positive actions you can take to encourage more business by referral:

Commit to your Forum, support your colleagues, and be there.

Introduce new faces to your Forum

Educate via one to one (121) engagement and regular presentation

Offer to help your colleagues

Give testimonials to services completed

Turn up early, stay a little longer

Who do I know who could use a little more business?

_____

_____

_____

_____

You've been with me thus far. So there are no prizes in understanding that by neglecting the needs of others, turning up for the food and hunting (as opposed to cultivating) the business are not ideal prorities for enhancing your business prospects, certainly at The Weekly Business Forum.

Here are another six actions that hinder referral:

Consistently arrive late for your Forum appointment (do you have something more important?)

Lack of engagement with others (my needs are more important!)

Presentations 'on the fly'

Hunting for the business

Neglecting to follow up on a given referral and

... failure to deliver what you say you will do

I'd like to meet the following professions at my Forum:

_____

_____

_____

_____

Essentially the messages you consistently deliver at your Forum are how others will see you or your business or your service.

Reliable or not?

Supportive or selling?

Hunter or cultivator?

Ask yourself how would you prefer to be regarded amongst your peers?

> *"Excellence is not a skill.
> It's an attitude."*
>
> ~ Ralph Marston

Your 60 second presentation

On a regular basis you are going to be asked to offer an insight into your business.

Generally you will only have a short time to deliver the message of needs and wants, so we need to be consider the content of the presentation.

It may consist of something like this:

1. THE NAME OF YOUR COMPANY
2. WHERE YOU ARE LOCATED
3. YOUR SPECIALIST SERVICE
4. THE SIGNS OF A GOOD REFERRAL FOR YOU?
5. YOU CAN CONTACT ME ON ...
6. YOUR MESSAGE LASTS WITH
   ... A MEMORY HOOK

The memory hook has been utilised by many established companies and does exactly as the name implies. People remember you through a catchy sign off.

For instance, do you remember these? Who/what companies were they signature lines of?

I'm loving it!
  Nice to see you, to see you nice.
Just like that!!
  Or perhaps ...
I don't belieeeve it!
  Just do it!
Or maybe ... You're fired!

"people buy from people"

~ The Weekly Business

Is it a referral?

So you happen to receive an enquiry during conversation and it appears to be a product or service that one of your network colleagues can help with. Our instinct is to pass the prospect your colleagues card.

The feeling is positive – it always is when we find that we are able to help someone, it's a natural instinct and can be a potent fulfilment to networking.

Something to ask the prospect though, as you pass the card:

As you pass on your Forum partners' card in recommendation ... simply ask:

"Would you take a call from my colleague?"

By simply asking this question the prospect understands that he/she should be receiving a call from someone who can offer a solution. It's a simple qualification of need, a very important part of referral generation and often overlooked.

Don't forget the referral follow-up

After all, your colleague has done the hard work. He/she have put the word in for you, identified the need and suggested a meeting – to which your prospect has agreed.

We understand that relations and civil protocol are to the fore when meeting new connections. It's the same when following up the referral although we must remember we're not following up to sell or ask for the order – there is still a way to go yet.

Before you make contact, do some homework. Check the locality, go to the web site and find out a little more about the company, who they work with and what their core business activity might be.

When making the call, be sure to mention your colleague who introduced you, this offers familiarity and common ground. Ask for a mutually beneficial time to meet up, then simply leave it at that, the more detail you need to impart, the better it is delivered face to face.

Before the actual meeting (if there is time), drop him/her an email to confirm the meeting, place and time and confirm his/her mobile number if applicable.

Here are one or two things to think about when making the initial connection:

* Remember it's about beginning a new relationship
* We're calling to better understand the prospect and to get the prospect to more fully understand us, as well as our business
* The purpose of our contact is to follow up the initial enquiry, not to sell but to determine the next level of action
* We should be listening to the prospect and when the time is right introducing our products or services, when we are invited to do so

Essentially the invitation to follow up on a referral should be done within **48hours** of receipt of the enquiry.

This is the start, and then of course there is the follow up and consolidation when most importantly we do as we say we are going to do.

> *"The secret of business is to know something that nobody else knows."*
>
> ~ Aristotle Onassis

(Forum meeting document as at June 2015)

The Weekly Business @ Northumberland

Welcome...*

Today's Agenda

Introduction to The Weekly Business

Education

Snapshot presentations from individuals in the room

How we intend to grow

Featured presentation

Network updates

Business round-up

- Who in the room would you like to know better? (Book a 121 meeting.)
- Have you heard something you may be able to offer help with?
- During the presentations today, did you hear the opportunity for a business lead?
- Perhaps you have been working on a referral for someone?
- Maybe you'd like to offer a verbal (or written) testimonial to one of your colleagues?

Close

* Doors open half hour before the meeting.

(Forum meeting document as at June 2015)

The Weekly Business @ Northumberland

'people buy from people'

What's it all about?

We're a diverse group of local businesses meeting regularly to develop our contacts. Our aim is to develop our business through affinity, recommendation and word of mouth referral.

Do I have to be a member?

No, we encourage the individual to recognise the value of regular attendance in developing trust and ultimately business relationships. We particularly welcome those with limited experience or understanding of the benefits that regular networking may bring. To this end, we feel the format to our meeting is an ideal introduction.

How much does attendance cost?

The venue hire levy varies per establishment. Either breakfast/lunch or light refreshment is included.
There is no 'membership fee'.

What might I expect on arrival?

Essentially you will be meeting people looking to hear about your business. You should aim to arrive 15 minutes prior the start of the regular structured meeting when introductions over tea/coffee take place. The formal meeting follows the same familiar routine each time we meet, finishing with enough time to book the engagement afterwards.

Am I expected to participate?

We want to hear about you and your business. Everyone attending is given to opportunity of introducing him/herself. We need to get to know you if we are to recommend your services.

What do I need to bring with me?

Apart from your business cards, a pen and paper would be useful. Of course, anyone else you feel may be interested in our forum is welcome although it is always wise to check with us first to ensure his/her business is not already represented.

How do I find the venue?

Each venue offers plenty of parking and a central location. Check with your meeting organiser beforehand if you have any special requirements.

If in any doubt go to Google maps, or visit the web via http://weeklybusiness-northumberland.co.uk or simply call us.

Is that it?

That's it. The rest is up to you.

(Forum meeting document as at June 2015)

The Weekly Business @
Northumberland

Your guidelines to how your 'Biz' Forum can best help you...

Communicating

We need to know you are attending the meeting; we look forward to your seeing you and cater for your presence. Keeping us informed of whether you CANNOT make The Weekly Business (Weeklybiz) is important. Getting in touch the evening beforehand (latest) is the least we'd expect.

Reserving your seat and Attendance

Once you have completed three visits to Weeklybiz your particular category of business is locked out to others. Please remember, your NET does not WORK if you do not regularly attend. Our meetings and consequently your business are poorer for your lack of attendance. Attending 50% of the available time is the minimum you need to allow in commitment and support of referral business. We do of course allow for life considerations, holidays and sickness etc. Although if we cannot see you regularly, then after consultation with you and in the best interests of the Forum we would search for a similar business to your own for support.

Cross Forum cultivation

Each Weeklybiz Forum has it's own culture defined by regular attendees developing business. You need to be aware that to visit an alternative meeting to that of your own should be by invitation only and of course there should be no clash of business interest when simple protocol is observed. The question of choice when 'giving' referral has often brought up when individuals maintain multiple seats and so regular visits outside of your own 'patch' are discouraged. With multiple representatives from the same company it works – not so for the individual "Forum hopper."

Timekeeping

Doors open half an hour prior the meeting although some turn up for business well in advance of this. The formal part of the meeting commences over refreshments and concludes after the business round up when open networking continues and most of the engagement/follow up takes place.

Participating

Communicating and turning up is a good start and getting to know your fellow attendees is where your business will start to benefit. We need to get to know each other before the confidence is instilled to pass lead and referral. Therefore supporting your Forum by turning up in good time, guest mentoring, helping at sign-in, supporting your Chair while working on your presentations and not forgetting one-to-one (121) with fellow attendees are fundamental and key to your success.

Tips for better business include:

- Practice, practice and rehearse again your presentation to offer clarity in what you do.
- Be specific with referral requests. Offer focus as to how we can help you.
- Take the extended presentation when you can. That's when we see *'the bigger picture.'*
- Bring a guest. Nothing is more valuable in terms of referral than a visitor.
- Book the 121 session with your colleagues, find out who they are, who they know.
- Remember to relax, you are amongst friends. Be comfortable in your own shoes...

(Forum meeting document as at June 2015)

The Weekly Business @ Northumberland

Getting to know you, or The Essential One to One (121)

It is essential to understand that if we are serious about providing referrals, we need to know who it is or what it is each of us are looking for and where we may be able to find it. By learning more about the person in business we have a better chance of success:

Below is a suggested start to your 121. Who is going to begin?

How do you usually find new business?

Are you receiving substantial new business from your business Forum?

If not, why do you think this is and what do you think would enhance your prospects?

Do you believe your 60 second presentation is doing the job of helping your colleagues understand your quest for new business?

How can I personally help you find referrals?

Where would your new clients or prospects normally be found?

What sort of questions should I be asking a potential prospect for your business?

Given our Network partners are our prospective 'sales force' what professions would you like to see complementing the existing Forum? What type of business or profession would they be?

A) _____

B) _____

C) _____

> *"When opportunity knocks, open the door."*
>
> ~ Anon

When the Baker met the Lawyer

Johannes (Hans) Volk is a friend of mine going back some 30 years. Born in Holland, he moved to Sydney Australia in his early twenties. This is where we first met.

I was alighting a home-bound train one evening, making my way up stairs to the car pack when the door at the top of the said stairs opened with a plume of white dust followed by a fellow covered in flour from shorts to clogs. Definitely Dutch our Hans.

You may have guessed, Hans back then worked as a pastry cook. Hans is still a mate, has a ready smile and enjoys life to the full. Hans has always been renowned for his BBQ and all that goes with it - needless to say we get on pretty well when we do meet up, which is not often enough these days. The same with any good friends I'm sure.

Hans and I travelled a bit thereafter and I ended up making plans to return to the UK, Hans spent some time in the Americas and word came back that he was 'smitten.' Hans had found the 'woman of his dreams in a recent trip stateside and was intent on winning her hand.

Of course others and myself had heard all the bravado before although it seemed Hans was intent and had made up his mind to sell up house in Sydney (which eventually, he did) and return to the USA and 'consolidate' (his words friends, not mine.)

Upon arrival in Chicago our Hans was invited to meet the prospective father-in-law, a prominent figure in Law circles and a high profile city slicker! This is where Hans and his prospects were to be shaken slightly ...

"No daughter of mine, who by the way is doing very well as a Solicitor, is to marry a pastry-cook!

"If you are serious about taking my daughters hand we'll have to get you into management. Is that understood?"

Now I don't know how you'd react? Must have been true love because Hans accepted the guidance of prospective bigwig father-in law. After some months he was then introduced to 'certain circles,' where he met up with someone who had introduced himself as a catering supplies provider.

Now Hans was a pastry cook, so he knew the trade of course and was certainly interested.

"What is it I need to do?" Hans enquired.

"We're looking for someone to help with sales."

Pretty soon Hans found himself immersed in the world of catering equipment supplies and spent the first twelve-months 'consolidating' in a different kind of way. Hans still considers himself by no means a 'natural' and he still proudly maintains his Dutch accent ...

The story goes that Hans is some twelve months into 'the job' and finding it tough going until he attended yet another trade fair and introduced himself and company to a buyer for a particular burger-chain.

The burger chain ended up being McDonalds and Hans, being Hans and using his skills soon found himself the preferred supplier of kitchenware for the famous (infamous?) restaurant chain USA-wide and eventually taking business globally.

The introduction, connection persistence and consolidation had worked for Hans. His resolve had paid off, connections had worked the magic and the 'luck he needed' came about by a combination of all of the above and a ready smile.

Hans still lives in Chicago with Susan, he visits Sydney every now and then during his business travels and whenever we speak I'm reminded of the guy who followed up his instincts and never gave up on pursuing what he wanted.

Networking is not for everyone, that's true. Although anyone looking for success in business should give networking some quality time and by investing in people the magic (such as Hans experience) may just happen for them.

Further copies of "Networking ... a guide" are available direct from the Publisher:

GO! Publicity.me (UK)

Telephone +44 1665 577084
charliekenny.wordpress.com

Or you can download a digital version by visiting Amazon or Lulu.com

~

During the Autumn a follow up to this edition will be available:

"Networking - a story"

www.ingramcontent.com/pod-product-compliance
Lightning Source LLC
Chambersburg PA
CBHW072252170526
45158CB00003BA/1066